Skeletal structure
for bone study p. 78

Multiplication tables p 84, 85
Subtraction & Addition tables p 80 -83
US
World } outline maps
Getting to Know you p. 45
Clean Desk Inspection- p. 21

TEACHER-TESTED TIMESAVERS

by
Imogene Forte

Incentive Publications, Inc.
Nashville, Tennessee

ISBN 0-86530-066-6

Illustrated by Gayle Seaberg Harvey
Cover by Tony Novak
Edited by Sally Sharpe

Table of Contents

ABOUT THIS BOOK

Teachers everywhere agree there's never enough time in the day to do everything that needs to be done! TEACHER-TESTED TIMESAVERS, created to help today's busy teacher save time and energy and alleviate stress and worry, contains all of the records, charts, forms, awards, certificates, incentives, patterns and other helpful aids necessary for creating an attractive, efficient and stimulating classroom. All of the materials in this book are ready to reproduce and use for instant results. The book has been divided into three sections to help you quickly and easily locate exactly what you need.

- **Awards, Subject Matter Incentives & Motivators**
  This section provides you with all of the motivational materials you need to keep students excited about learning. Included are awards and certificates for every occasion and many subjects, attractive reading motivators and unique bookmarks, classroom helper badges, seasonal and holiday name tags, "customized" stationery, creative doorknob communicators, subject banners and mini-patterns, and motivational activities such as dinosaur finger puppets and creative story starters.

- **Records, Charts, Forms & Fact Sheets**
  This section contains all of the reproducibles necessary for establishing an organized and efficient classroom as well as helpful fact sheets and informative materials every teacher needs. Get to know your students and their individual strengths and weaknesses by using the student questionnaire, student profile, and student goals work sheet. Get organized and stay that way all year long by using the classroom charts, class roll, substitute teacher's daily schedule, and homework assignment sheet. Establish good communication channels by utilizing the class newsletter and parent conference forms. Give students the guidance they need in conducting special studies by distributing individualized study forms and outline guides for specific topics . . . and use the bonus "fact sheets" in creative ways to enhance and enrich learning in different subject areas.

- **Calendar Art, Seasonal Mini-Patterns, Bulletin Boards & Recipes**
This section supplies you with ready-to-reproduce patterns and materials that will transform your classroom into the most attractive and beneficial learning environment it can be. Each of nine monthly calendars is followed by a page of seasonal mini-patterns to be used in conjunction with the calendars as well as for bulletin boards, displays, classroom decorations, and much more. You'll never run out of new ways to use the monthly banners and weekday headers, and you'll find literally hundreds of creative uses for the "fold, trace and cut" patterns. Two "fold, trace and cut" patterns are included for each month as well as illustrated examples of many different uses. Finally, two pages of some of the best simple recipes for art supplies and tasty treats are included for your easy reference time and time again!

This timesaving resource contains all of the essentials and all of the extras you need to produce the extraordinary results you want without the extra time and expense. No one will ever guess it was so easy!

AWARDS, SUBJECT MATTER INCENTIVES & MOTIVATORS

PLANT TENDER

CENTER KEEPER

LIBRARY HELPER

CLASSROOM ☆HELPER☆

HALL MONITOR

LUNCHROOM ★HELPER★

CHALKBOARD TENDER

ART TABLE TENDER

TEACHER'S HELPER

COMPUTER CHECKER

Helper badges
© 1989 by Incentive Publications, Inc., Nashville, TN.

TEACHER NOTES

From: The Teacher's Desk

To: _____

A Special Message For You!

FROM YOUR TEACHER!

DOORKNOB COMMUNICATORS

Cut these festive doorknob communicators out of construction paper, wallpaper, foil or felt. The possibilities are endless — homework assignments, special messages, holiday or seasonal decorations, etc.

DON'T FORGET!

Just A Reminder . . .

_____

_____

_____

_____

_____

_____   _____
signed   date

News Worth Noting

_____

_____

_____

_____

_____

_____

_____

CONGRATULATIONS!

To: _____

For: _____

From: _____

date

Happy Birthday _____ !

_____ is a great age.

signed _____

date _____

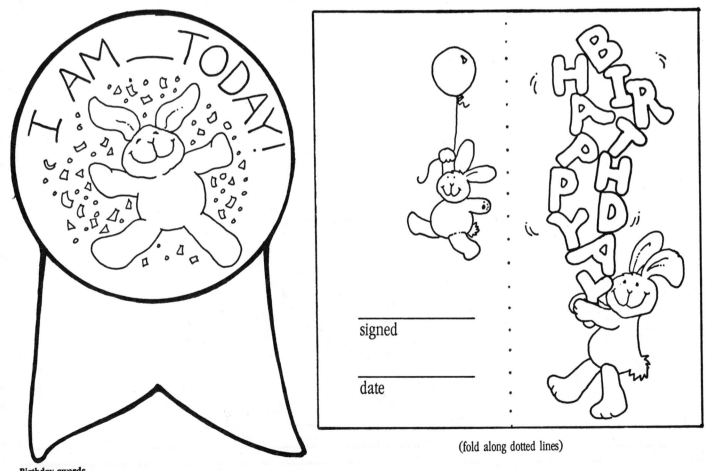

I AM ___ TODAY!

signed _____

date _____

(fold along dotted lines)

Birthday awards

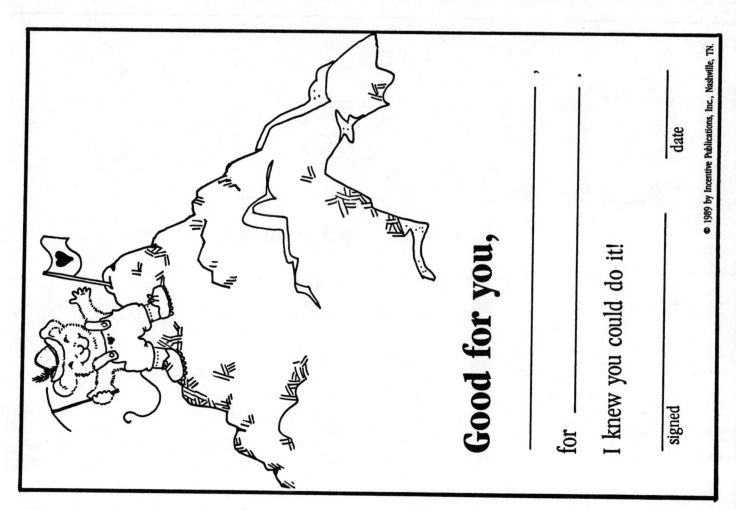

Good for you,

for _____

I knew you could do it!

signed _____

date _____

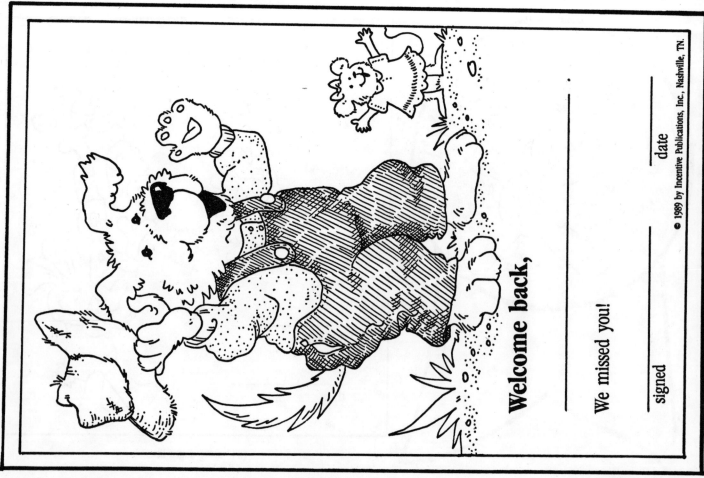

Welcome back,

We missed you!

signed _____

date _____

Purr-fect Attendance Award

To: _____

signed _____   date _____

First Place Award

To: _____

signed _____

date _____

Best Homework of the Day Award

To: _____

For: _____

☆ signed _____

date _____

Sharp Pencil Award

To: _____

For: _____

signed _____   date _____

GOOD CITIZENSHIP AWARD

To: _____

For: _____

_____

_____
signed   date

The Clean Desk Award Is Presented To:

_____

for passing the clean desk inspection!

_____   _____
signed   date

Good and Healthy Award

To: _____

For: _____

signed _____ date _____

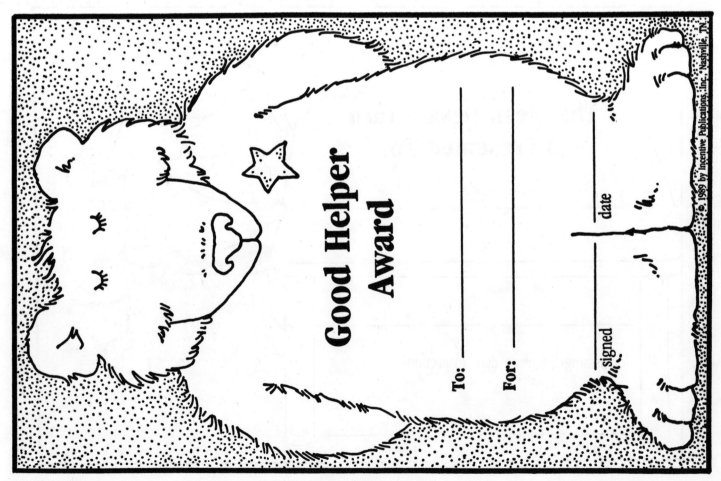

Good Helper Award

To: _____

For: _____

signed _____ date _____

Good Grooming Award

To: _____

For: _____

_____

_____
signed

_____
date

Today was a good day

for _____

because _____

_____.

_____
signed

_____
date

Super Scientist
Award

To: _____

For: _____

_____

_____
signed

_____
date

Mighty Math Award

To: _____

For: _____

_____

_____
signed

_____
date

is a computer champ!

signed _____ date _____

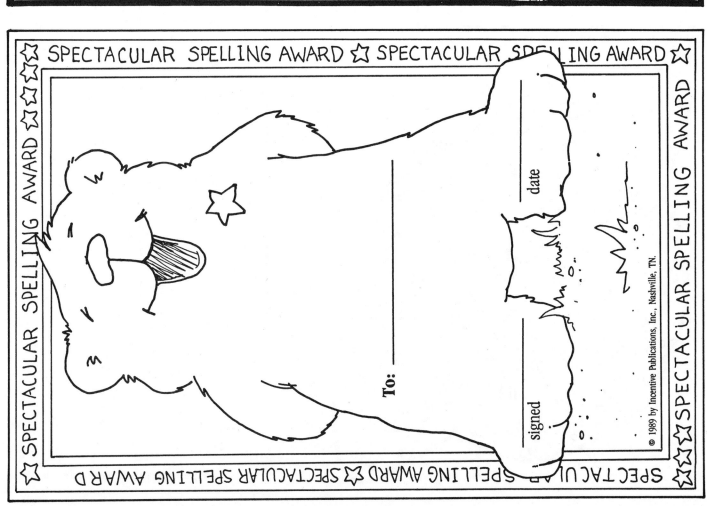

SPECTACULAR SPELLING AWARD ☆ SPECTACULAR SPELLING AWARD ☆

To: _____

date _____

signed _____

READING/LANGUAGE ARTS MOTIVATORS

READING RECORD

Name

Title	Date

This mini reading record may be slipped into library book pockets!

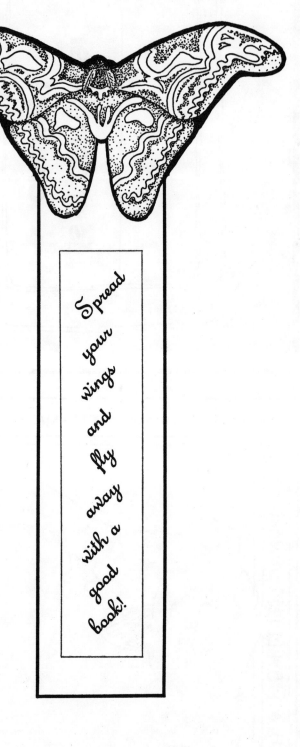

Spread your wings and fly away with a good book!

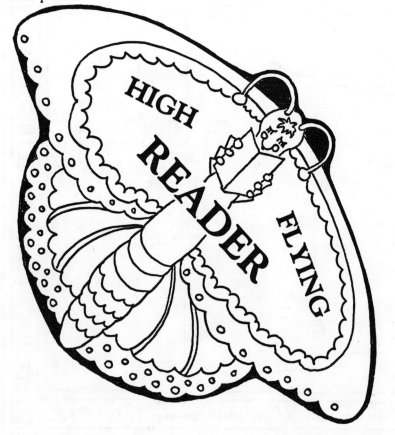

HIGH FLYING READER

Bookworm Award

To: _____

For reading _____ books.

_____
signed

_____
date

This book belongs to

_____

I AM A BOOKWORM ♥ I READ, READ, READ!

SUPER SPELLER

I FINISHED MY BOOK!

CLASS HISTORIAN

POET OF RENOWN

WORD WIZARD

Reading/language arts motivators
© 1989 by Incentive Publications, Inc., Nashville, TN.

HOMEWORK BOOK MARKERS

SCIENCE

THIS WEEK'S SPELLING

READING ASSIGNMENT

SOCIAL STUDIES

cut along the dotted lines

Name tags

Name tags
© 1989 by Incentive Publications, Inc., Nashville, TN.

Science

Social Studies

Reading & Writing

Math

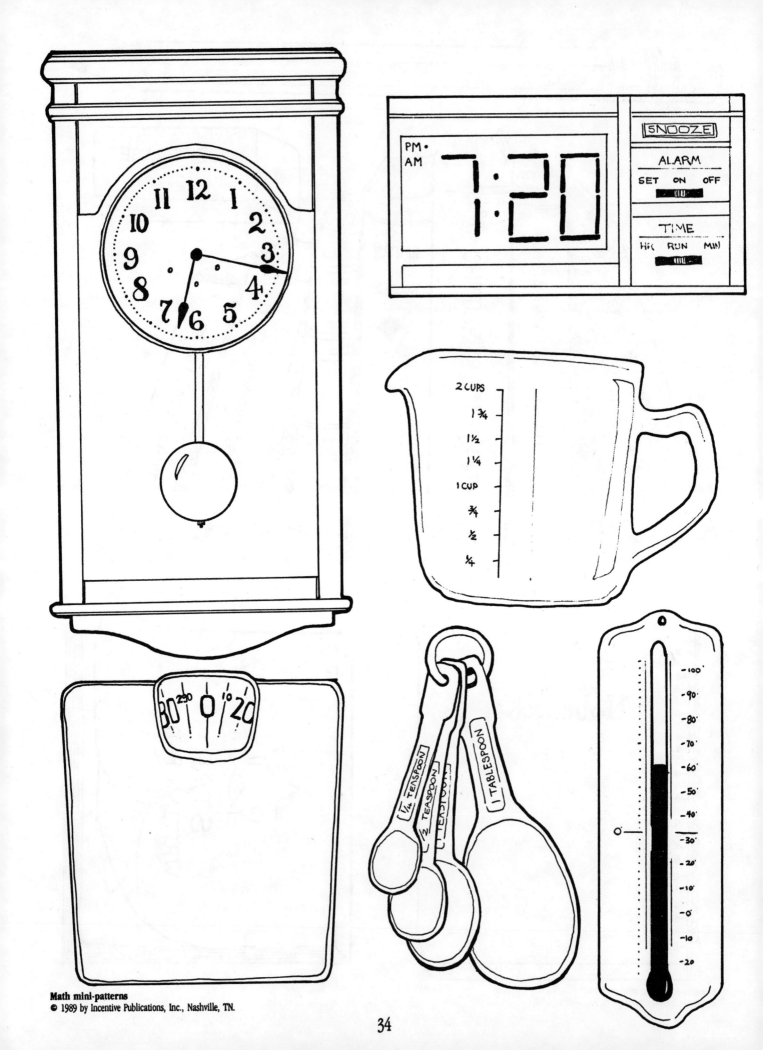

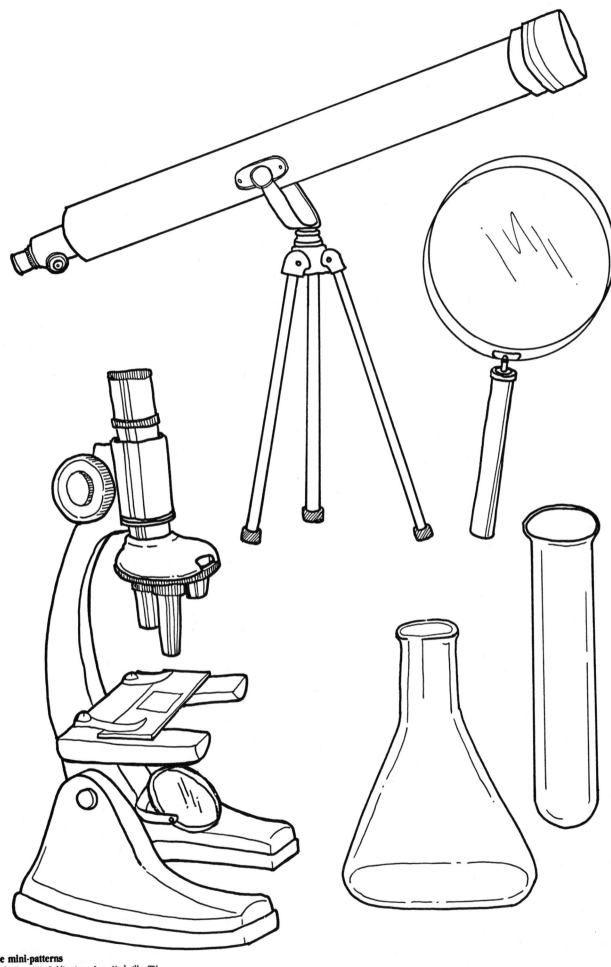

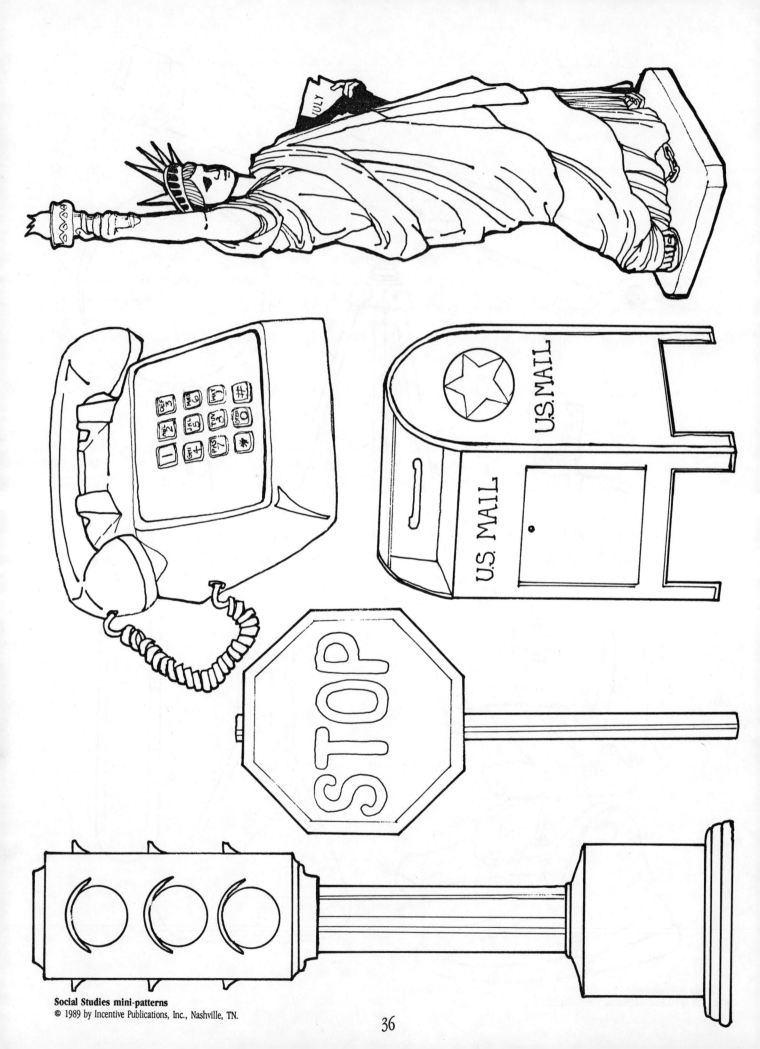

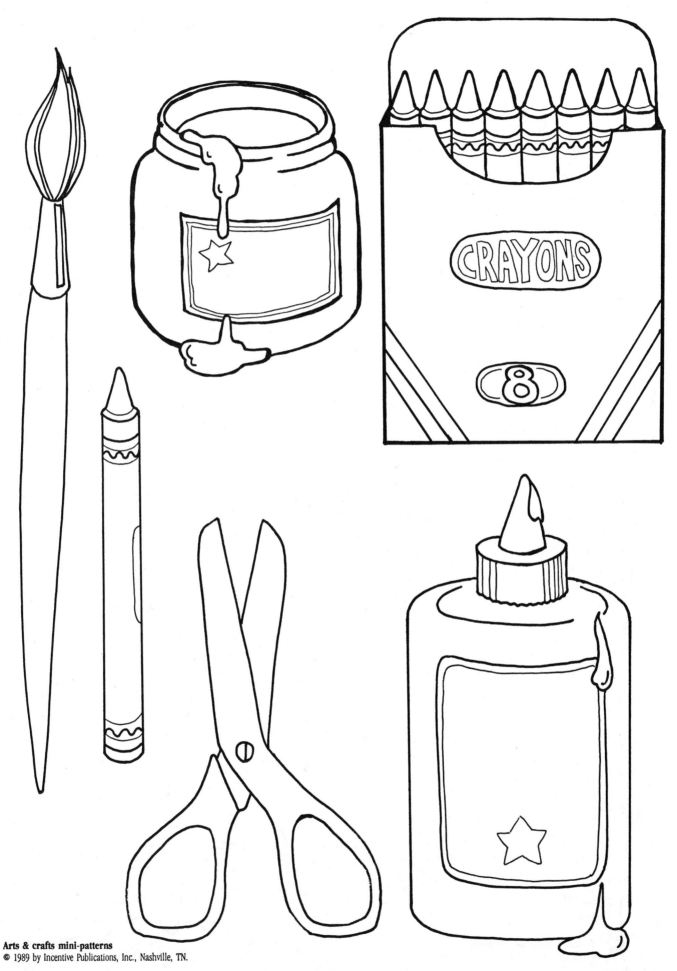

CRAYONS

8

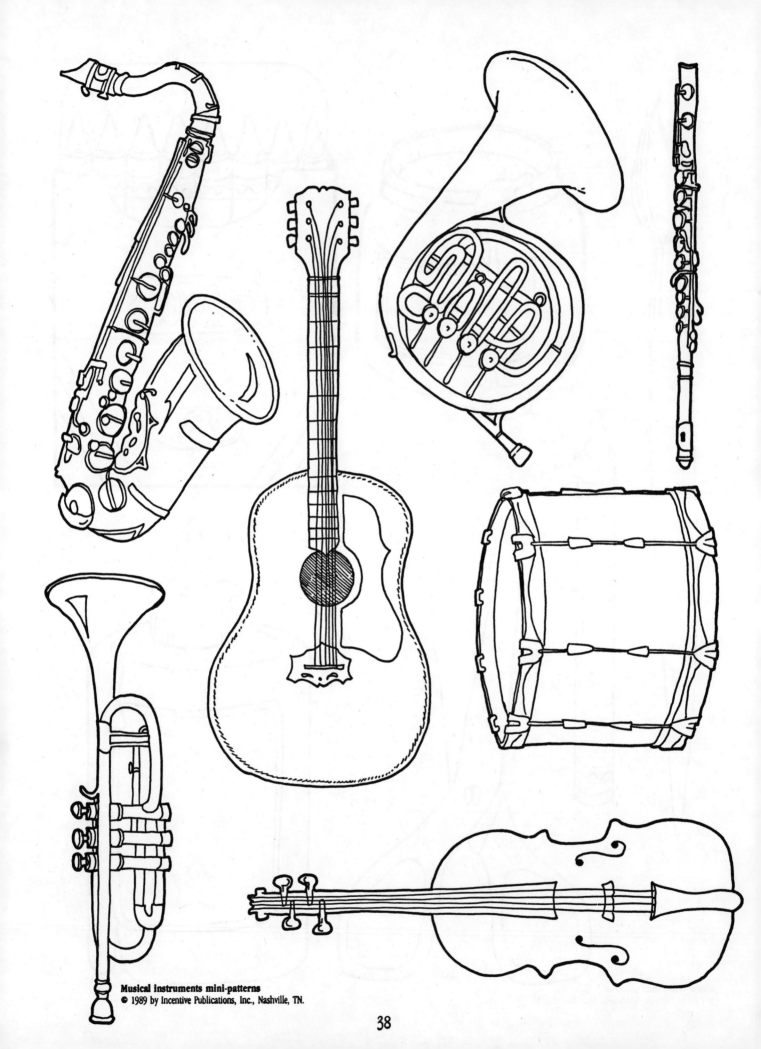

Musical instruments mini-patterns
© 1989 by Incentive Publications, Inc., Nashville, TN.

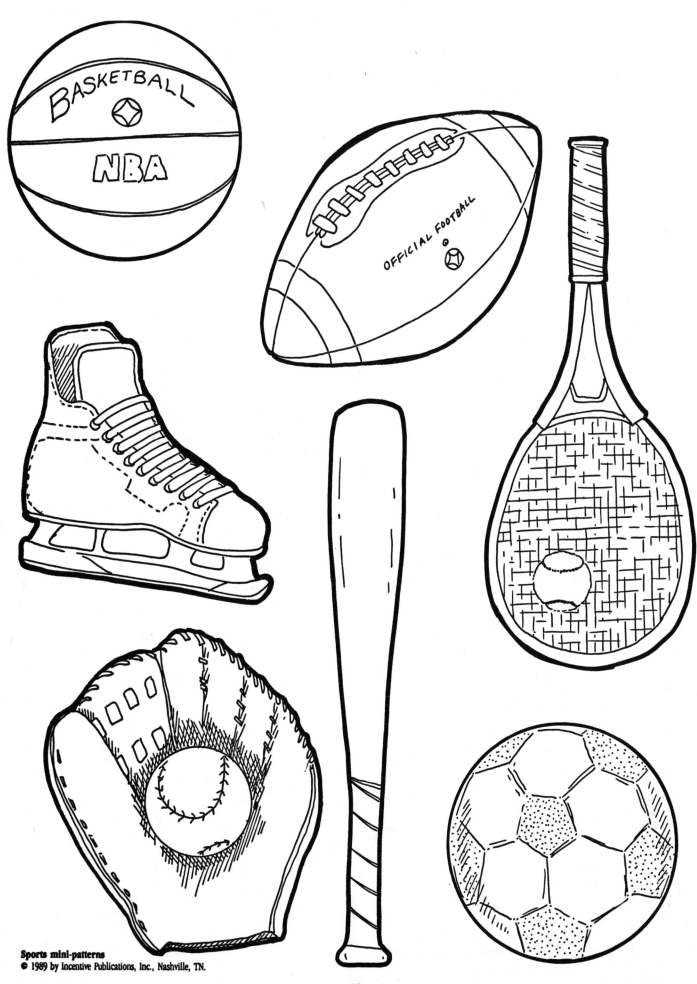

BASKETBALL
NBA

OFFICIAL FOOTBALL

Sports mini-patterns
© 1989 by Incentive Publications, Inc., Nashville, TN.

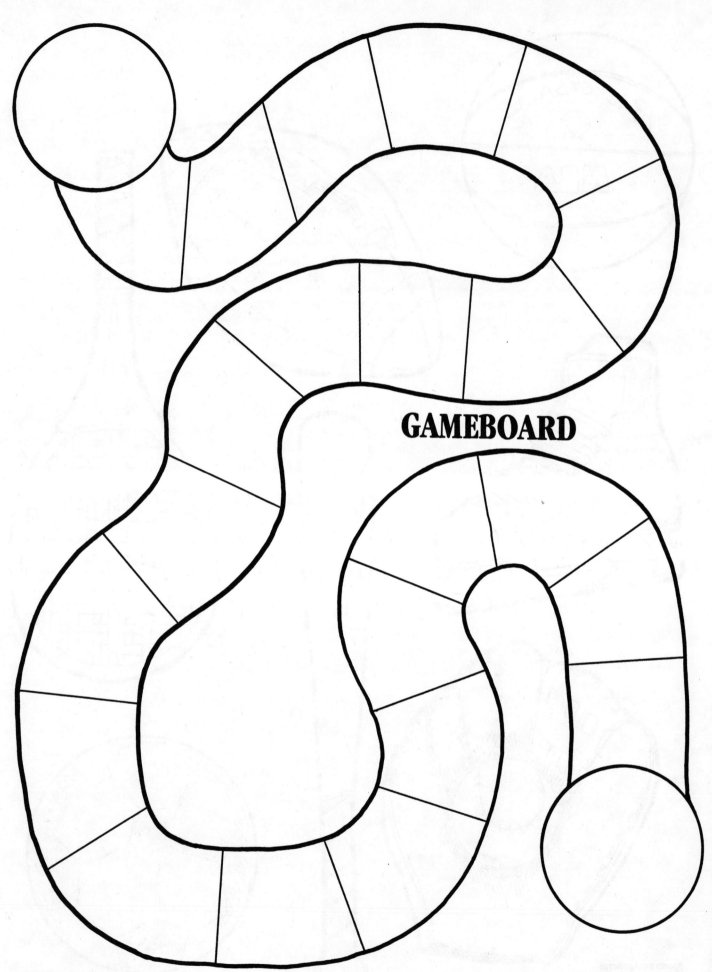

GAMEBOARD

DANCING DINOSAURS

Color and cut out the finger puppets.
Make up your own play and be ready to present it to the class

tape

CREATIVE STORY STARTERS

1. Just as the clock struck twelve . . .

2. Suddenly, we heard the strangest noise coming from nowhere . . .

3. I never should have opened the door . . .

4. Just around the corner . . .

5. The principal threw open the classroom door . . .

6. The whole class roared with laughter when . . .

7. A giant redbird circled overhead . . .

8. A very old man with a crooked cane came to the door . . .

9. The house had ninety-seven rooms, one hundred and two doors and . . .

10. The magic egg began to crack . . .

11. If I had three wishes, I would wish for . . .

12. Even though the sign read "No Trespassing" . . .

13. Someone had tied a pink ribbon on the baby elephant's tail . . .

14. We never intended to cause so much trouble . . .

15. The clowns began to cry . . .

16. A hundred years ago today . . .

17. The wolf howled forlornly and . . .

18. As the spaceship came closer . . .

19. The zookeeper opened the tiger's cage . . .

20. As the train roared through the darkness . . .

RECORDS, CHARTS, FORMS & FACT SHEETS

GETTING TO KNOW YOU

Name _____

Please help me to get to know you by completing the sentences below.
This information will help me to plan activities and projects that will be interesting and helpful to you during the school year.
Read all of the sentences before beginning to write.
Then write the first thought that comes to your mind as you reread each sentence.

1. The one thing I like best about school is _____

   _____ .

2. The one thing I would like to change most about this school is _____

   _____ .

3. The one thing I hope for most this year is _____

   _____ .

4. The one thing I hope that my teacher will do this year is _____

   _____ .

5. The one thing I hope that my teacher will not do this year is _____

   _____ .

6. The subject I find easiest is _____ .

7. The subject I find hardest is _____ .

8. The thing I liked best about my last year's teacher was _____

   _____ .

9. This year I would like to make improvements in _____

   _____ .

My name is _____ .

I look something like this.

This is something that makes me happy.

This is something that makes me sad.

MY GOALS FOR THE DAY

Name _____ Date _____

Goal	Done	Teacher's Comment

Today I worked _____.

I feel _____.

Tomorrow I would like to _____.

CLASSROOM CHART

QUICK-CHECK CHART
FOR STUDENT OBSERVATION

Week of _____

Student	Monday	Tuesday	Wednesday	Thursday	Friday

SUBSTITUTE TEACHER'S
DAILY SCHEDULE

Time	Activity	Materials, Textbooks, and Page Numbers

Have a great day!
Please leave notes about the day here:

CLASS ROLL

BOYS

1. _____
2. _____
3. _____
4. _____
5. _____
6. _____
7. _____
8. _____
9. _____
10. _____
11. _____
12. _____
13. _____
14. _____
15. _____

GIRLS

1. _____
2. _____
3. _____
4. _____
5. _____
6. _____
7. _____
8. _____
9. _____
10. _____
11. _____
12. _____
13. _____
14. _____
15. _____

HOMEWORK ASSIGNMENTS

Name _____ Week of _____

MONDAY
Reading _____
Math _____
Science _____
Social Studies _____
Spelling _____
Special _____

TUESDAY
Reading _____
Math _____
Science _____
Social Studies _____
Spelling _____
Special _____

WEDNESDAY
Reading _____
Math _____
Science _____
Social Studies _____
Spelling _____
Special _____

THURSDAY
Reading _____
Math _____
Science _____
Social Studies _____
Spelling _____
Special _____

FRIDAY
Reading _____
Math _____
Science _____
Social Studies _____
Spelling _____
Special _____

News From Our Class

Date:

We Are Learning About . . .

Special Events

Our Calendar

Classroom Update

PARENT CONFERENCE FORM

Dear _____ ,

I would like to schedule a conference to discuss your child's progress on

_____

at _____ .

Please let me know if this time is convenient for you.

_____
Teacher

----- (cut along dotted lines) --

Please complete the appropriate response and return.

_____ Yes, I will be able to come for a conference on _____

at _____ .

_____ No, I will not be able to

come for a conference on _____

at _____ . A better time would be

_____ at _____ .

_____
Parent

INDEPENDENT STUDY PLAN

Name: _____

Topic of study: _____

   I.   I want to find answers for these questions:

       _____

       _____

       _____

  II.   This is my plan of study:

       _____

       _____

       _____

 III.   I will need these materials:

       at school: at home:

       _____   _____

       _____   _____

       _____   _____

 IV.   This is how I will share my results: _____

       date of completion: _____ date for sharing: _____

       plan for sharing: _____

       _____

       _____

This is to Certify that

has completed all the work associated with the

Independent Study of:

_____

on this the _____ day of _____ , 19 ___

and is hereby declared a member of

_____ Independent Workers' Club

The _____

And is entitled to all the privileges thereof.

_____
signed

A PLAN FOR INDIVIDUALIZED SPELLING

Teacher Preparation

- You will need a spelling list or old spelling workbooks containing words for the appropriate grade level (also one or two grades above and below).
- Make a list of new or difficult words from subject areas, units, literature, seasons, holidays, etc. Add to this list often.
- Keep a running list on 3" x 5" cards of words individual students misspell on daily papers.
- You will need a spiral notebook or file box for each student.

Procedure

Monday

Make sure that each student has his or her notebook and lists of:

- words missed the previous week
- words misspelled on daily papers
- words from subjects, seasons, etc.
- words from an individual grade level list

You may choose to add selected words from the dictionary.

Tuesday

Use the words in activities such as games, puzzles, mazes, unfinished sentences, spelling bees, etc.

Wednesday

Have a trial test. To provide variety, students may work in pairs and give each other words orally.

Thursday

Have the students look up words in the dictionary and practice spelling and using the words (place special emphasis on more difficult words).

Friday

Have a spelling test. (You may want to have students test each other.) Correct the papers or arrange for the students to correct them. Instruct each student to write the words he or she missed on next week's list. Add specific words to each student's list.

Teacher Notes

- Some modifications of this plan may be desirable to make it "fit" individual classrooms. In instances where grade level spelling books and/or workbooks are required for each student, these materials may be incorporated into an individualized program.
- Avoid repetition, drill and meaningless work sheets or board work. Use attractive work sheets, creative games and writing projects instead of the expected routine assignments.

RHYMING WORDS

ade: blade, fade, glade, grade, laid, made, maid, paid, raid, wade

and: band, brand, canned, fanned, gland, grand, hand, land, sand, stand

are: bar, car, far, jar, mar, tar, scar

ate: bait, date, fate, gate, hate, late, mate, rate, state, wait

ball: call, crawl, fall, gall, hall, mall, stall, tall, wall

bare: bear, care, dare, fare, hair, pear, rare, stare, there, wear

bat: cat, fat, flat, hat, mat, pat, rat, sat, slat

beak: leak, meek, peak, peek, reek, seek, weak, week

bend: blend, end, lend, mend, pretend, rend, send, spend, tend

bin: din, fin, gin, kin, pin, sin, tin, win

black: back, crack, lack, pack, quack, rack, sack, smack, stack, track

block: clock, cock, dock, flock, knock, lock, mock, rock, sock, tock

blue: clue, crew, drew, few, flew, glue, knew, new, to, true

bold: bowled, cold, fold, gold, hold, mold, old, rolled, sold, told

bone: cone, known, lone, phone, stone, tone, zone

book: brook, cook, crook, hook, look, rook, took

bring: cling, ding, fling, king, sing, sling, ring, wing

bunk: clunk, drunk, dunk, hunk, junk, punk, stunk, sunk, trunk

burn: churn, earn, fern, learn, stern, turn, yearn

by: cry, eye, fry, high, I, lie, pie, sigh, tie, why

can: ban, fan, man, pan, ran, tan, van

cane: gain, lain, main, pain, plane, rain, stain, train, vain

cap: clap, flap, gap, lap, map, nap, slap, tap, trap, wrap

chive: dive, drive, five, hive, jive, live

clay: gay, hay, lay, may, play, ray, say, tray, way

clean: bean, dean, glean, green, keen, lean, mean, seen, teen

cog: dog, flog, fog, frog, hog, jog, smog

core: door, floor, four, more, pour, roar, sore, store, tore, wore

cream: dream, gleam, seam, steam, team

dale: fail, gale, hale, jail, male, nail, pale, rail, sale, tale

dear: deer, fear, hear, here, near, peer, queer, rear, steer, year

dine: fine, line, mine, nine, pine, sign, swine, tine, vine, whine

dish: fish, squish, swish, wish

FROM THE LIBRARY OF

Fill the library shelves by writing the titles of books and the dates you finish reading them on the books below.

NON-FICTION

FICTION

BOOKS TOO GOOD TO MISS!

READING RECORD

Name _____

Date	Title of Book	Pages Read	New and Different Words
1.			
2.			
3.			
4.			
5.			
6.			
7.			
8.			
9.			

HOME READING RECORD

Name _____

How To Use This Record:
Enter the title, author and date started for each book.
After reading a book, share the book with a family member and rate the book together.
Ask the family member to initial the chart in the space provided.

Rating Scale

	great book	fairly good book	uninteresting book
	☆	○	✕

Title	Author	Date Started	Date Shared	Rating	Family Member's Initials

BOOK REPORT PYRAMID

Name _____

Start at the bottom of the pyramid and work your way up to the top.

How

Why

What

When

Where

Who

Author

Name of Book

GUIDE FOR STUDYING THE LIFE OF A PERSON

Person's name: _____

Time of person's life: _____

Place where person lived: _____

Person's early life (parents, home, school, hobbies, etc.):	Person's later life (home, occupation, life style, accomplishments):
_____	_____
_____	_____
_____	_____
_____	_____
_____	_____

Why person is remembered: _____

_____

_____

Brief biographical summary of the person's life and accomplishments: _____

_____

_____

_____

_____
Name

_____
Date

GUIDE FOR STUDYING
A STATE OR PROVINCE

Name of state or province: _____

_____

Sketch of state or province:	Physical features (mountains, plains, bodies of water, deserts, hills, etc.):

Brief statement of history (first settlers, where they came from, why they came, etc.):

_____

_____

Natural resources: _____

_____

Life today (major cities, characteristics, major industries, etc.): _____

_____

_____

Events, celebrations, and other special features: _____

_____

_____   _____

Name   Date

GUIDE FOR STUDYING A COUNTRY

Name of country: _____

Sketch of country:	Physical features (size, shape, location):

Brief statement of early history (when, where, how, and by whom it was settled):

_____

_____

_____

Was the country governed by another country at one time? _____

If so, name the mother country: _____

Is the country now independent? _____

Name three well-known people from the country:

1. _____ known for _____ .

2. _____ known for _____ .

3. _____ known for _____ .

_____   _____

Name   Date

SOCIAL STUDIES
PROJECT PLAN

Topic:

_____

Type of Project:

_____

_____

Date to begin: _____ Date to finish: _____

Books and resources needed:

_____

_____

_____

Study plan:

_____

_____

Method of presenting project:

_____

_____

_____
Name

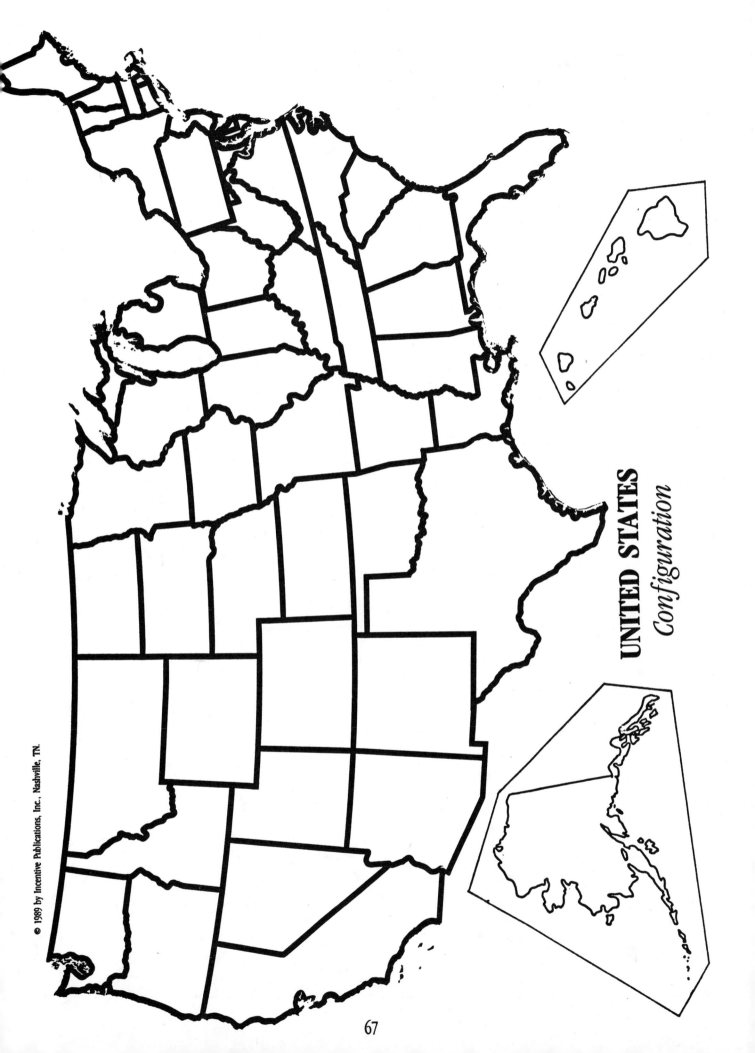

UNITED STATES *Configuration*

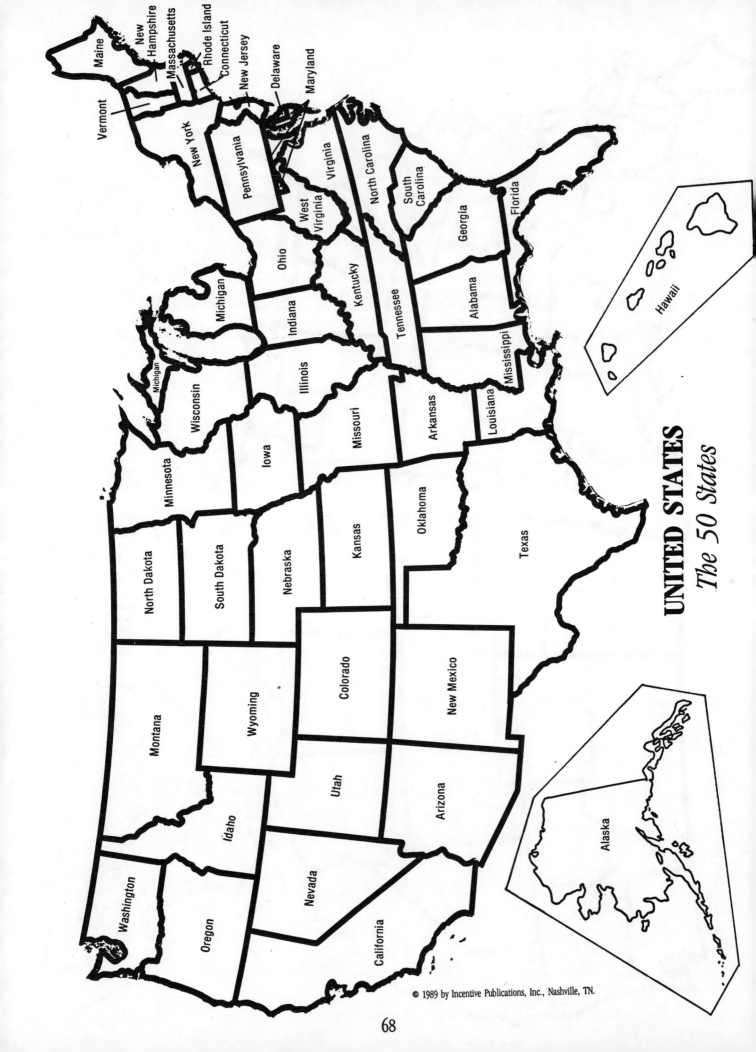

UNITED STATES
The 50 States

Maine
New Hampshire
Massachusetts
Rhode Island
Connecticut
New Jersey
Delaware
Maryland
Vermont
New York
Pennsylvania
Virginia
North Carolina
South Carolina
Florida
West Virginia
Ohio
Kentucky
Tennessee
Georgia
Alabama
Michigan
Indiana
Illinois
Michigan
Wisconsin
Missouri
Arkansas
Louisiana
Mississippi
Minnesota
Oklahoma
Texas
North Dakota
South Dakota
Nebraska
Kansas
Colorado
New Mexico
Montana
Wyoming
Utah
Arizona
Idaho
Nevada
Washington
Oregon
California
Hawaii
Alaska

© 1989 by Incentive Publications, Inc., Nashville, TN.

UNITED STATES
States & Capitals

Augusta, ME
Concord, NH
Boston, MA
Providence, RI
Hartford, CT
Trenton, NJ
Dover, DE
Annapolis, MD
Montpelier, VT
Albany, NY
Harrisburg, PA
Charleston, WV
Richmond, VA
Raleigh, NC
Columbia, SC
Tallahassee, FL
Columbus, OH
Frankfort, KY
Atlanta, GA
Lansing, MI
Nashville, TN
Montgomery, AL
Indianapolis, IN
Springfield, IL
Jackson, MS
Madison, WI
Jefferson City, MO
Little Rock, AR
Baton Rouge, LA
St. Paul, MN
Des Moines, IA
Topeka, KS
Oklahoma City, OK
Austin, TX
Bismarck, ND
Lincoln, NE
Pierre, SD
Denver, CO
Santa Fe, NM
Cheyenne, WY
Helena, MT
Salt Lake City, UT
Phoenix, AZ
Boise, ID
Carson City, NV
Olympia, WA
Salem, OR
Sacramento, CA

Honolulu, HI

Juneau, AK

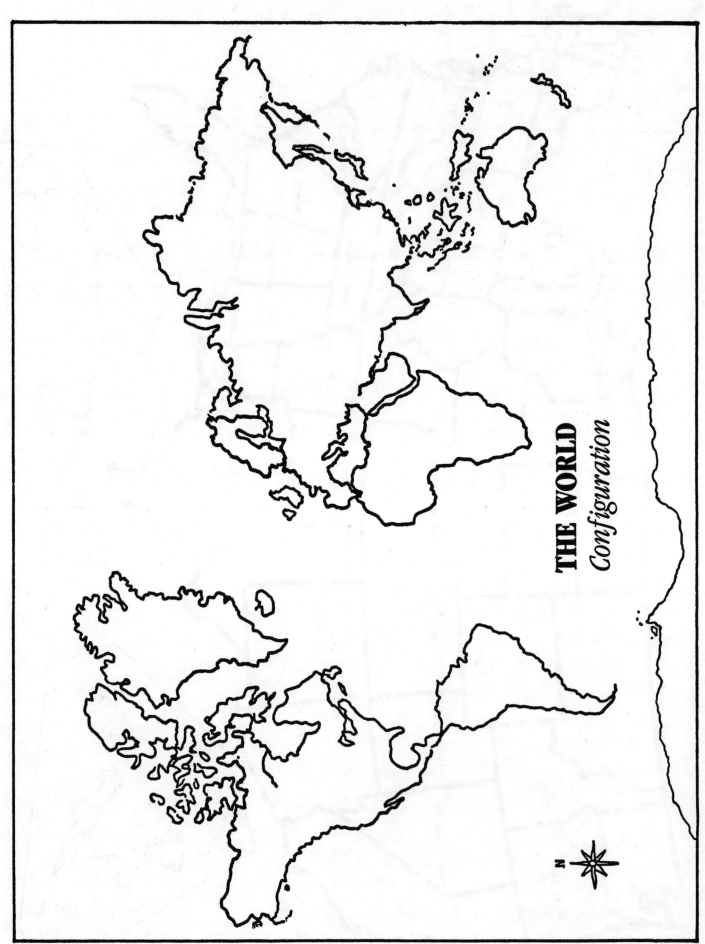

THE WORLD
Configuration

N

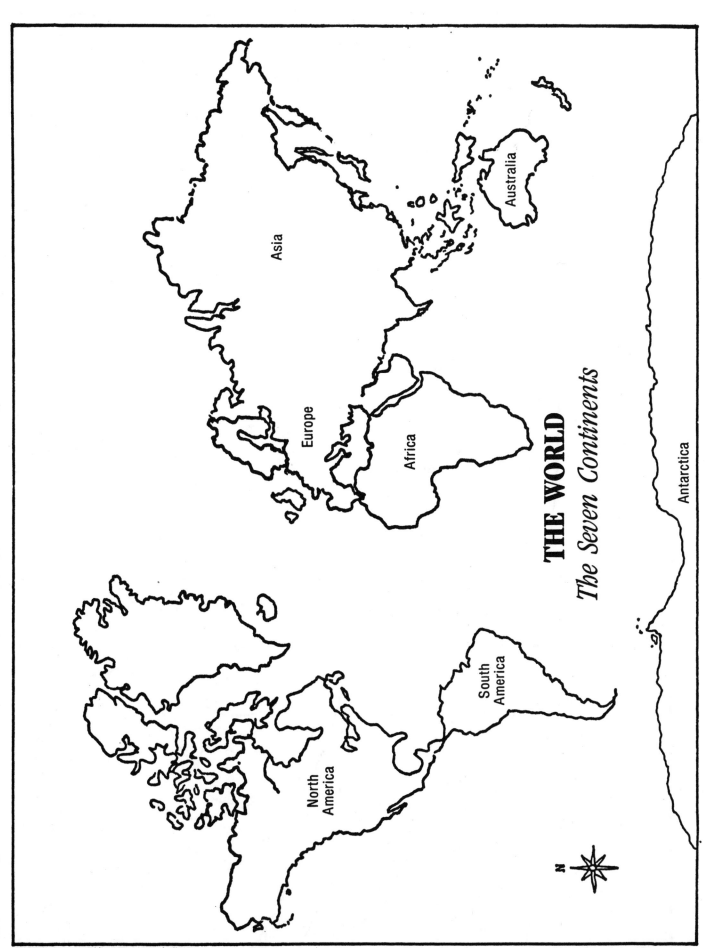

THE WORLD
The Seven Continents

Asia

Australia

Europe

Africa

Antarctica

North America

South America

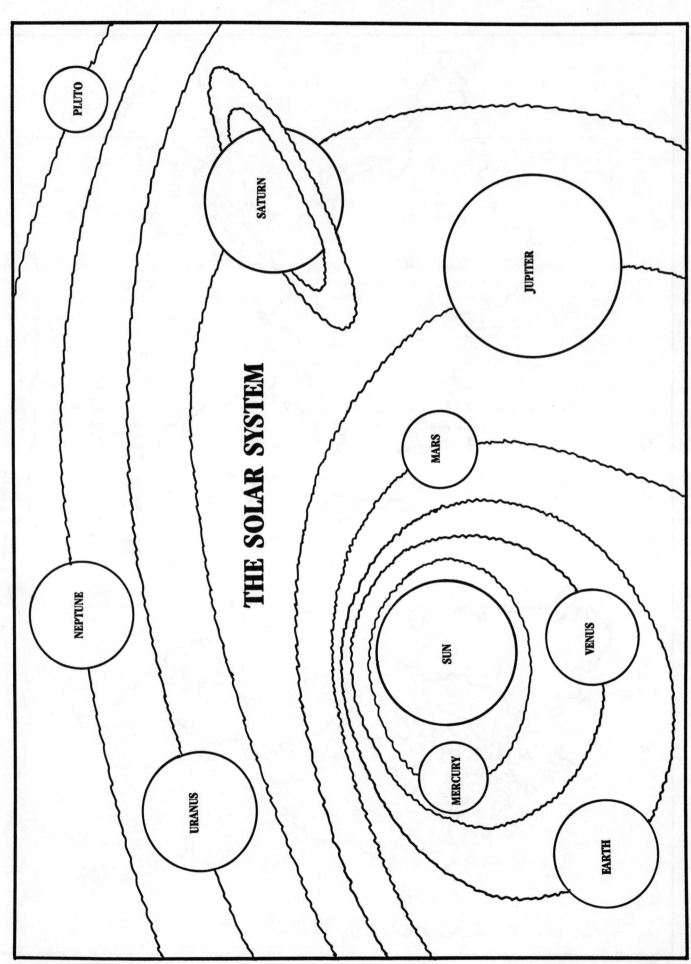

THE SOLAR SYSTEM

PLUTO

SATURN

JUPITER

MARS

NEPTUNE

SUN

VENUS

MERCURY

URANUS

EARTH

THE SUN & THE PLANETS

NEPTUNE

MERCURY

PLUTO

JUPITER

VENUS

URANUS

SATURN

MARS

EARTH

SUN

SCIENCE EXPERIMENT OUTLINE

Name _____

Materials: _____

_____

_____

Procedure: _____

_____

_____

_____

Data:

Date	What I Did	What I Observed
_____	_____	_____
_____	_____	_____
_____	_____	_____

Conclusions: _____

_____

_____

_____

Findings: _____

_____

_____

Evaluation (including what I could have done differently and *how* it would have affected the experiment): _____

_____

_____

_____

GUIDE FOR OBSERVING A PLANT

Name _____ Date _____

Name the plant: _____

Look at the plant and identify its main parts.
Briefly describe each part in the spaces below.
(You may not be able to see each part on every plant.)

Part	Color	Shape	Size	Texture
Flower				
Fruit				
Leaves				
Stem				
Root				

Did the plant grow from a seed, bulb, or another like plant? _____
(You may not be able to tell. If not, guess and research your answer later.)

Can any part of the plant be eaten by human beings? _____

If so, which part(s) may be eaten?　　_____ stem　　_____ leaf
　　　　　　　　　　　　　　　　　　_____ seeds　　_____ root
　　　　　　　　　　　　　　　　　　_____ flower　　_____ fruit

Does any part of the plant have a distinct odor? _____

If the plant has a fruit or an edible root, feel it and describe how it feels (waxy, spongy, firm, prickly, slippery, rough, smooth, limp, crisp, etc.).

_____

_____

Use the back of this page to draw a sketch or sketches of the plant.

GUIDE FOR OBSERVING AN ANIMAL

Name _____ Date _____

Animal's Name: _____

Physical Appearance

Describe its body surface: color: _____

texture: _____

Number of main body parts: _____

Number of legs (if any): _____

Habits

How does the animal move? _____

What does it like to eat? _____

Where does it live? _____

How does it communicate through sound? _____

How does it communicate through movement? _____

How and when does it rest? _____

What excites the animal or causes it to become active? _____

_____

How does it defend itself?

Appearance: _____

Natural weapon: _____
(sting, bite, claws, odor, etc.)

How does it relate to human beings? _____

_____

How does it relate to its own kind? _____

_____

GUIDE FOR STUDYING
AN ENDANGERED ANIMAL

Animal's Name: _____

Sketch of animal:	Physical features (size, number of legs, skin covering, etc.):

Animal's natural habitat: _____

_____

Animal's distinguishing habits (food, migration, mating, etc.): _____

_____

_____

Major cause of present danger: _____

_____

Steps to be taken to protect the animal: _____

_____

Organizations to contact for information: _____

_____

_____

_____   _____
Name   Date

SKELETAL STRUCTURE

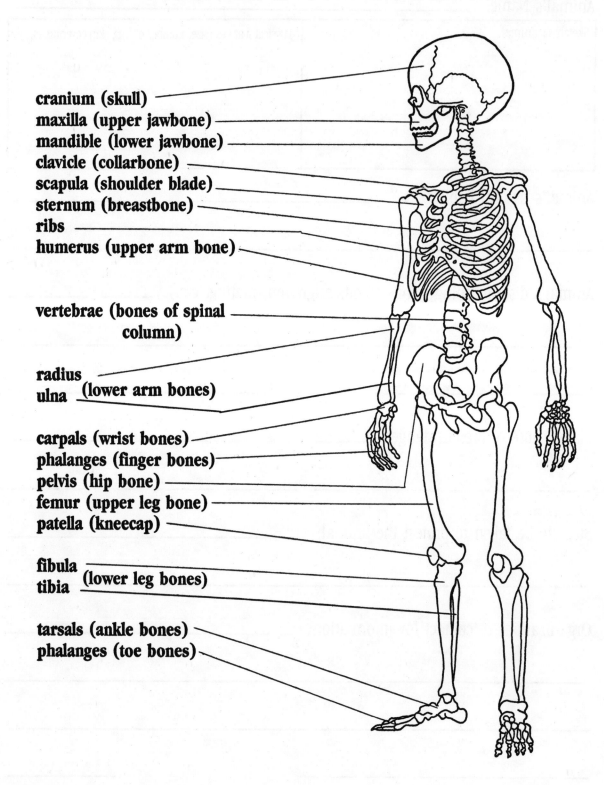

cranium (skull)
maxilla (upper jawbone)
mandible (lower jawbone)
clavicle (collarbone)
scapula (shoulder blade)
sternum (breastbone)
ribs
humerus (upper arm bone)

vertebrae (bones of spinal column)

radius
ulna (lower arm bones)

carpals (wrist bones)
phalanges (finger bones)
pelvis (hip bone)
femur (upper leg bone)
patella (kneecap)

fibula
tibia (lower leg bones)

tarsals (ankle bones)
phalanges (toe bones)

COMPUTER TERMS

1. Bug - a mistake in a computer program

2. Computer - an electronic machine which stores instructions and information, processes the instructions and information, performs tasks or calculations, and displays the "results" on a screen

3. Cursor - the symbol which shows where input will appear on the screen

4. Data - information put into or received from a computer

5. Debug - to find and correct mistakes in a computer program

6. Disk - stores programs and data when the computer is turned off

7. Input - to put data and instructions into a computer

8. Interface - the way one communicates with a computer (monitors, keyboards, mice and printers are interface devices)

9. Keyboard - a typewriter-like device with rows of keys which is used to type information into the computer

10. Memory - circuits in the computer which hold data and programs while the computer is working on them

11. Menu - a list on the computer screen from which one may make selections

12. Monitor - the computer screen

13. Mouse - a device used to move the cursor around on the screen

14. Output - information a computer prints out or displays on a screen; information stored in memory

15. Printer - a machine which prints output

16. Program - instructions given to a computer

17. Software - computer programs, usually found on disks, tapes or cards

18. Terminal - a device which displays input and output (usually located separately from the computer itself and generally consisting of a keyboard and monitor)

ADDITION PRACTICE TABLE

Name _____

+	0	1	2	3	4	5	6	7	8	9	10	11	12
0	0	1	2	3	4	5	6	7	8	9	10	11	12
1	1	2	3	4	5	6	7	8	9	10	11	12	13
2	2	3	4	5	6	7	8	9	10	11	12	13	14
3	3	4	5	6	7	8	9	10	11	12	13	14	15
4	4	5	6	7	8	9	10	11	12	13	14	15	16
5	5	6	7	8	9	10	11	12	13	14	15	16	17
6	6	7	8	9	10	11	12	13	14	15	16	17	18
7	7	8.	9	10	11	12	13	14	15	16	17	18	19
8	8	9	10	11	12	13	14	15	16	17	18	19	20
9	9	10	11	12	13	14	15	16	17	18	19	20	21
10	10	11	12	13	14	15	16	17	18	19	20	21	22
11	11	12	13	14	15	16	17	18	19	20	21	22	23
12	12	13	14	15	16	17	18	19	20	21	22	23	24

ADDITION TABLE WORK SHEET

Name _____

+	0	1	2	3	4	5	6	7	8	9	10	11	12
0													
1													
2													
3													
4													
5													
6													
7													
8													
9													
10													
11													
12													

SUBTRACTION PRACTICE TABLE

Name _____

−	13	14	15	16	17	18	19	20	21	22	23	24	25
0	13	14	15	16	17	18	19	20	21	22	23	24	25
1	12	13	14	15	16	17	18	19	20	21	22	23	24
2	11	12	13	14	15	16	17	18	19	20	21	22	23
3	10	11	12	13	14	15	16	17	18	19	20	21	22
4	9	10	11	12	13	14	15	16	17	18	19	20	21
5	8	9	10	11	12	13	14	15	16	17	18	19	20
6	7	8	9	10	11	12	13	14	15	16	17	18	19
7	6	7	8	9	10	11	12	13	14	15	16	17	18
8	5	6	7	8	9	10	11	12	13	14	15	16	17
9	4	5	6	7	8	9	10	11	12	13	14	15	16
10	3	4	5	6	7	8	9	10	11	12	13	14	15
11	2	3	4	5	6	7	8	9	10	11	12	13	14
12	1	2	3	4	5	6	7	8	9	10	11	12	13

SUBTRACTION
TABLE WORK SHEET

Name _____

−	13	14	15	16	17	18	19	20	21	22	23	24	25
0													
1													
2													
3													
4													
5													
6													
7													
8													
9													
10													
11													
12													

MULTIPLICATION
PRACTICE TABLE

Name _____

×	0	1	2	3	4	5	6	7	8	9	10	11	12
0	0	0	0	0	0	0	0	0	0	0	0	0	0
1	0	1	2	3	4	5	6	7	8	9	10	11	12
2	0	2	4	6	8	10	12	14	16	18	20	22	24
3	0	3	6	9	12	15	18	21	24	27	30	33	36
4	0	4	8	12	16	20	24	28	32	36	40	44	48
5	0	5	10	15	20	25	30	35	40	45	50	55	60
6	0	6	12	18	24	30	36	42	48	54	60	66	72
7	0	7	14	21	28	35	42	49	56	63	70	77	84
8	0	8	16	24	32	40	48	56	64	72	80	88	96
9	0	9	18	27	36	45	54	63	72	81	90	99	108
10	0	10	20	30	40	50	60	70	80	90	100	110	120
11	0	11	22	33	44	55	66	77	88	99	110	121	132
12	0	12	24	36	48	60	72	84	96	108	120	132	144

MULTIPLICATION TABLE WORK SHEET

Name _____

×	0	1	2	3	4	5	6	7	8	9	10	11	12
0													
1													
2													
3													
4													
5													
6													
7													
8													
9													
10													
11													
12													

TABLES OF MEASURES

Time

1 minute (min)	=	60 seconds (sec)	1 year (yr)	=	52 weeks
1 hour (hr)	=	60 minutes (min)	1 year (yr)	=	365 1/4 days
1 day	=	24 hours (hr)	1 decade	=	10 years
1 week	=	7 days	1 century	=	100 years

Weight

METRIC SYSTEM

1 gram (g)	=	1000 milligrams (mg)
1 kilogram (kg)	=	1000 grams (g)
1 metric ton (t)	=	1000 kilograms (kg)

ENGLISH SYSTEM

1 pound (lb)	=	16 ounces (oz)
1 ton (T)	=	2000 pounds (lb)

Length

METRIC SYSTEM

1 centimeter (cm)	=	10 millimeters (mm)
1 decimeter (dm)	=	10 centimeters (cm)
1 meter (m)	=	10 decimeters (dm)
1 meter (m)	=	100 centimeters (cm)
1 meter (m)	=	1000 millimeters (mm)
1 decameter (dkm)	=	10 meters (m)
1 hectometer (hm)	=	100 meters (m)
1 kilometer (km)	=	100 decameters (dkm)
1 kilometer (km)	=	1000 meters (m)

ENGLISH SYSTEM

1 foot (ft)	=	12 inches (in)
1 yard (yd)	=	36 inches (in)
1 yard (yd)	=	3 feet (ft)
1 mile (mi)	=	5280 feet (ft)
1 mile (mi)	=	1760 yards (yd)

Capacity

METRIC SYSTEM

1 teaspoon (t)	=	5 milliliters (mL)
1 tablespoon (T)	=	12.5 milliliters (mL)
1 liter (L)	=	1000 milliliters (mL)
1 liter (L)	=	1000 cubic centimeters (cm³)
1 liter (L)	=	1 cubic decimeter (dm³)
1 liter (L)	=	4 metric cups
1 kiloliter (kL)	=	1000 liters (L)

ENGLISH SYSTEM

1 tablespoon (T)	=	3 teaspoons (t)
1 cup (c)	=	16 tablespoons (T)
1 cup (c)	=	8 fluid ounces (fl oz)
1 pint (pt)	=	2 cups (c)
1 pint (pt)	=	16 fluid ounces (fl oz)
1 quart (qt)	=	4 cups (c)
1 quart (qt)	=	2 pints (pt)
1 quart (qt)	=	32 fluid ounces (fl oz)
1 gallon (gal)	=	16 cups (c)
1 gallon (gal)	=	8 pints (pt)
1 gallon (gal)	=	4 quarts (qt)
1 gallon (gal)	=	128 fluid ounces (fl oz)

CALENDAR ART, SEASONAL MINI-PATTERNS, BULLETIN BOARDS & RECIPES

SEPTEMBER 2

SUNDAY	MONDAY	TUESDAY	WEDNESDAY	THURSDAY	FRIDAY	SATURDAY

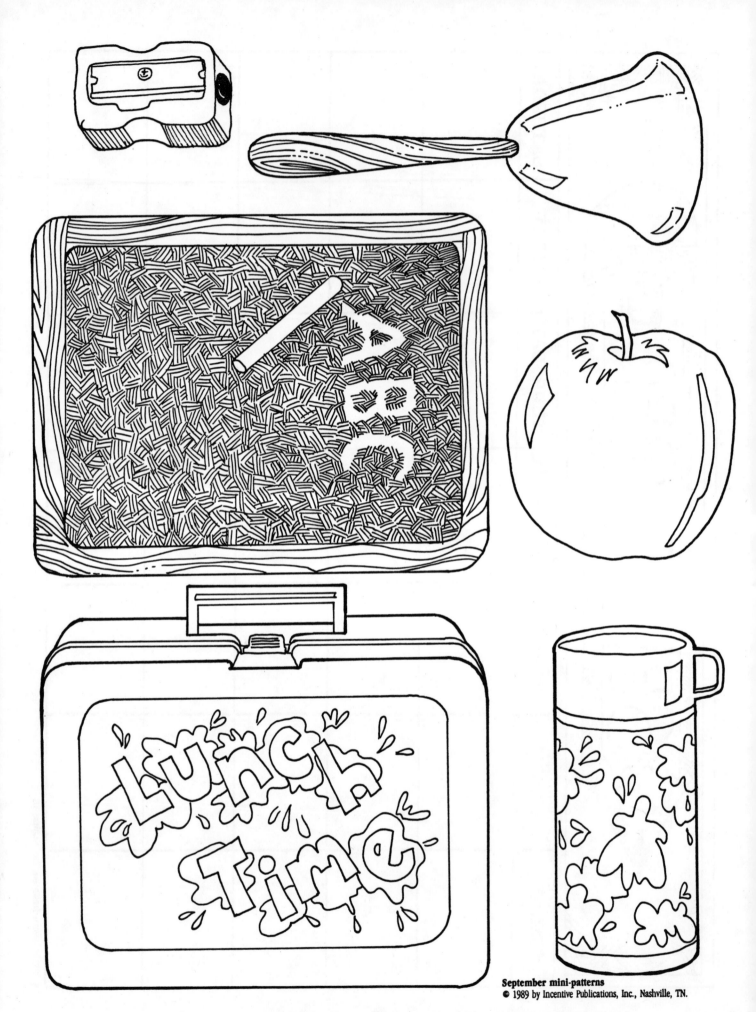

September mini-patterns
© 1989 by Incentive Publications, Inc., Nashville, TN.

OCTOBER

SUNDAY	MONDAY	TUESDAY	WEDNESDAY	THURSDAY	FRIDAY	SATURDAY

October mini-patterns

NOVEMBER

SUNDAY	MONDAY	TUESDAY	WEDNESDAY	THURSDAY	FRIDAY	SATURDAY

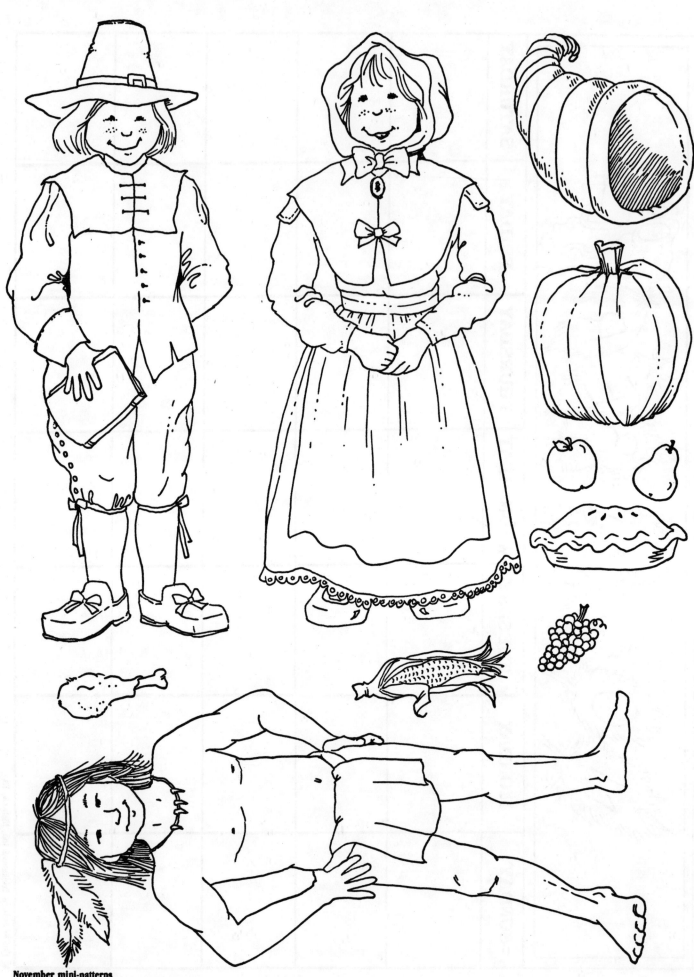

DECEMBER

SUNDAY	MONDAY	TUESDAY	WEDNESDAY	THURSDAY	FRIDAY	SATURDAY

December mini-patterns
© 1989 by Incentive Publications, Inc., Nashville, TN.

JANUARY

SUNDAY	MONDAY	TUESDAY	WEDNESDAY	THURSDAY	FRIDAY	SATURDAY

HAPPY NEW YEAR

NEW YEAR BABY

January mini-patterns
© 1989 by Incentive Publications, Inc., Nashville, TN.

FEBRUARY

SUNDAY	MONDAY	TUESDAY	WEDNESDAY	THURSDAY	FRIDAY	SATURDAY

MARCH

SUNDAY	MONDAY	TUESDAY	WEDNESDAY	THURSDAY	FRIDAY	SATURDAY

APRIL

SUNDAY	MONDAY	TUESDAY	WEDNESDAY	THURSDAY	FRIDAY	SATURDAY

April mini-patterns
© 1989 by Incentive Publications, Inc., Nashville, TN.

SUNDAY	MONDAY	TUESDAY	WEDNESDAY	THURSDAY	FRIDAY	SATURDAY

May mini-patterns
© 1989 by Incentive Publications, Inc., Nashville, TN.

SUNDAY	MONDAY	TUESDAY	WEDNESDAY	THURSDAY	FRIDAY	SATURDAY

June mini-patterns
© 1989 by Incentive Publications, Inc., Nashville, TN.

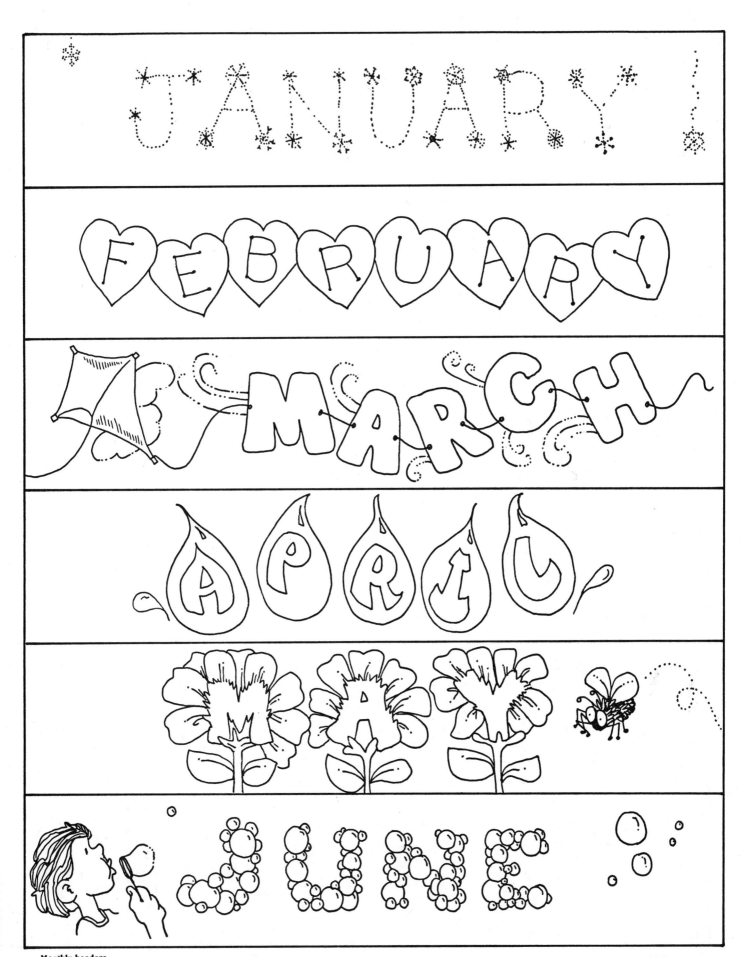

JANUARY !

FEBRUARY

MARCH

APRIL

MAY

JUNE

Monthly headers
© 1989 by Incentive Publicatons, Inc., Nashville, TN.

109

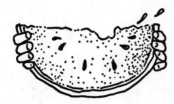
JULY

AUGUST

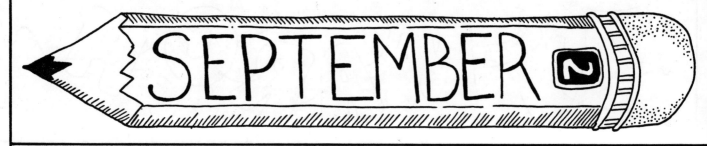
SEPTEMBER 2

OCTOBER

NOVEMBER

DECEMBER

Monthly headers

SUNDAY

MONDAY

TUESDAY

WEDNESDAY

THURSDAY

FRIDAY

SATURDAY

Days of the week headers
● 1989 by Incentive Publications, Inc., Nashville, TN.

FOLD, TRACE AND CUT PATTERNS

One, two, three — it's as simple as can be! The fold, trace and cut patterns on the following ten pages will decorate and enliven your classroom from September to June. The process is simple enough for even the very immature child to participate in and yet quick and easy enough to hold the interest of impatient middle graders. Once materials and patterns are in place, very little teacher time is required. With the simplest of instructions, students will be able to fold, trace and cut a multitude of classroom decorations and learning aids.

Once students have made decorations using the provided patterns, they will enjoy making original creations according to their own designs. Your classroom will virtually "come alive" with leaves and flowers native to your region; scary and friendly jack-o'-lanterns and snowmen; one-of-a-kind snowflakes; shiny stars; left and right hands and feet; trucks, cars, ships and planes; dinosaurs and kittens; and other marvelous creations of your students' imaginations!

To get started, gather the following items and place them in a basket: construction paper, gift-wrap, foil, tissue paper, colored pencils, scissors, and the patterns on the following ten pages. Follow the simple procedure outlined below to demonstrate the "construction" of the designs for the students. Refer to the next page and illustrate various uses of the designs. Then involve the students in making and using one fold, trace and cut pattern. As the year progresses, you may wish to "branch out" and experiment by using fabric, felt, wallpaper, mylar, plastic, newspaper, shelf paper, butcher paper, and other materials.

CONSTRUCTION

1. Reproduce the desired pattern, enlarging or reducing the pattern to suit your purpose.
2. Tape the pattern to the edge of a strip of construction paper at least as
   tall as the pattern.
3. Fold the strip of paper into an accordion fold that is the width of the
   pattern.
4. Cut out the pattern, taking care not to cut the dotted edges.
5. Unfold the pattern and cut as many as you need for the project.

3.

4.

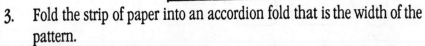

5.

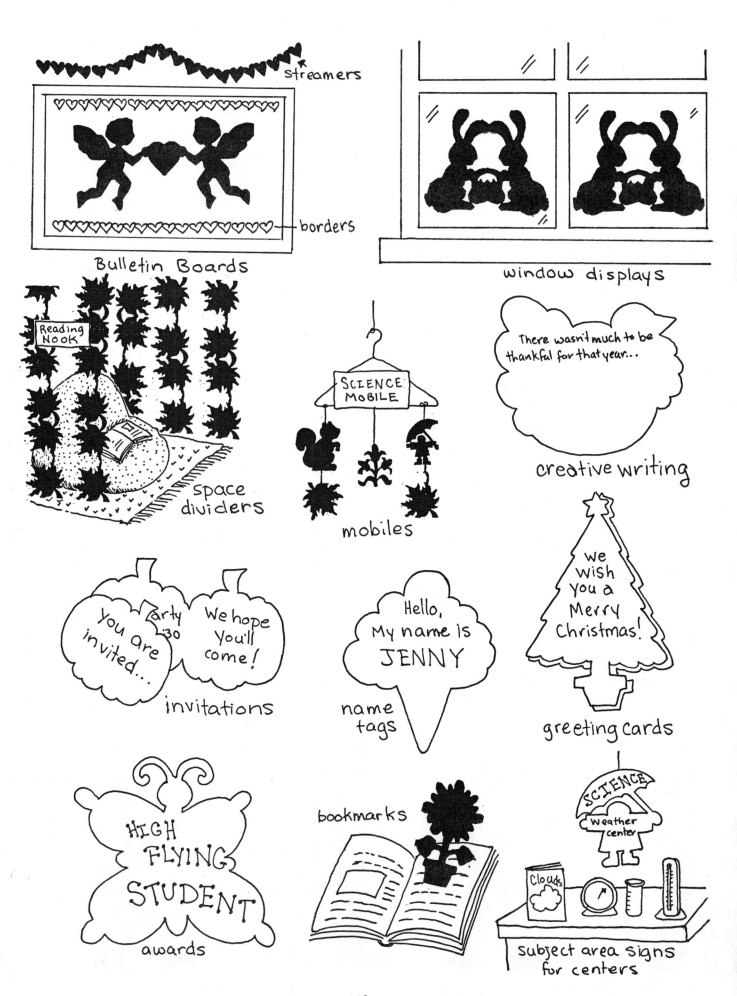

streamers

borders

Bulletin Boards

window displays

Reading Nook

space dividers

SCIENCE MOBILE

mobiles

There wasn't much to be thankful for that year...

creative writing

Party 30
You are invited...
We hope You'll come!

invitations

Hello, My name is JENNY

name tags

we wish you a Merry Christmas!

greeting cards

HIGH FLYING STUDENT

awards

bookmarks

SCIENCE
Weather center
Clouds

subject area signs for centers

SEPTEMBER

OCTOBER

NOVEMBER

DECEMBER

JANUARY

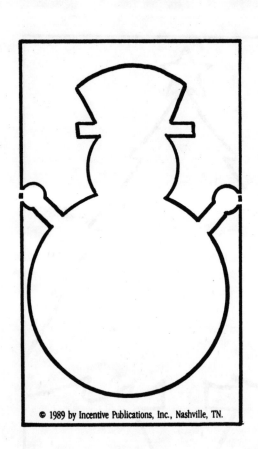

FEBRUARY

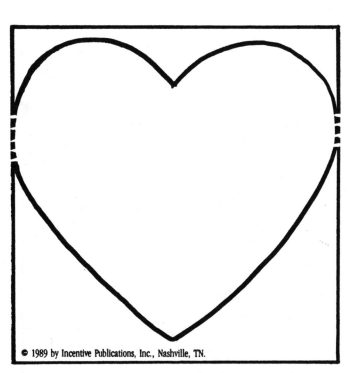

MARCH

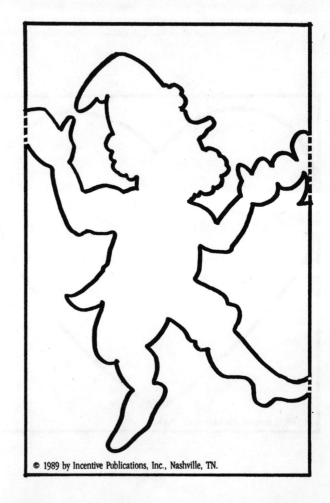

APRIL

MAY

JUNE

ARTFULLY EASY RECIPES FOR THE WHOLE YEAR

PASTE

1 cup water
½ cup flour
pinch of salt

Mix water and flour together slowly in a saucepan. Add salt and bring to a boil over low heat. Stir until thick and glossy.

PLAY DOUGH

1 cup flour
½ cup salt
1 cup water
1 tablespoon cooking oil
2 teaspoons cream of tartar

Mix and heat ingredients until a ball forms. Add a touch of food coloring if desired.

MAKE-BELIEVE MARBLE

1 cup white glue
½ cup water
plaster of Paris
tempera paint (liquid)

Put water in a container. Sprinkle plaster on water until a thick, creamy mixture forms. Add glue to plaster mixture. Drip some tempera over the plaster and stir until the mixture looks streaked. Pour into a mold and let harden.

CREATIVE CLASSROOM COOKERY WITHOUT A STOVE

Quick and Easy Krispy Treats

Materials:
electric skillet
spoon
baking pan

Ingredients:
1 tbs. butter
1 c miniature marshmallows
1 tsp. vanilla
1½ c rice or oat ring-shaped cereal

1. Using low heat and stirring constantly, melt the butter and marshmallows in the skillet.
2. Turn off heat and stir in vanilla. Fold in the cereal until it is completely coated.
3. Spread the cereal mixture in the baking pan.
4. Cut into squares after the mixture cools.

Peanut Butter Surprises

Materials:
measuring cup   waxed paper
large bowl   cookie sheet
wooden spoon

Ingredients:
1 c honey   1 c peanut butter
1 c rice cereal   1 c coconut
1 c dry milk

1. Measure the honey, rice cereal, dry milk and peanut butter into the bowl.
2. Stir with a wooden spoon until well mixed.
3. Spread the coconut on waxed paper.
4. Shape the dough mixture into small balls and roll in the coconut until covered on all sides.
5. Place the balls on the cookie sheet and place in the refrigerator for half an hour before serving.

INDEX